The Rhodesian War
in poetry

1965-1980

Matthew R Brackley

I remember the stillness
The discipline of quiet
I hold true to that today
Your training never goes away
It is locked in
Available for immediate use

If I could pick up a service rifle
I would know it blindfolded
The satisfying snap of the magazine
Your thumb knows the safety
Automatic memory

Jacket design and illustration
by Author

For all Rhodesians who served their country,
whether operationally or in a supporting role.
For the families
They too, bear the scars.
This collection of poems are hauntingly beautiful.
It is of a generation.

Poems

For our Fallen
Did I ever tell you?
That familiar quickening (Part I)
That familiar quickening (Part II)
The Bronze Cross
Casevac
To say goodbye
The widow
In the loss
In the dying moments
The souvenirs of war
The conscripted son
The flight of the Lynx
I ,was a Selous Scout
A Hunter was lost
African Moon
The Zambesi Valley
The faded camouflage
30 years later....
Aftermath
I remember the stillness
Where have they all gone?

For all Rhodesians who served their country,
whether operationally or in a supporting role.
For the families
They too, bear the scars.
This collection of poems are hauntingly beautiful.
It is of a generation.

Poems

For our Fallen

Every year
In November
I shed a tear
For our fallen
I will always remember

Rhodesia's lost generation
Gave their lives
Battles fought and won
Men died
Duty, done

I shed a tear
and sigh
The fighting men
of the Selous
The S.A.S
The R.L.I

A Rhodesia Regiment
Men of the R.A.R
The B.S.A.P
Internal Affairs
All who kept the country free
The enemy running...
As we dismount from the 'G car'

Remember the Blues
The casevacs
The uplifts ,aerial support
Parachuting from the Daks

Every year
In November
I shed a tear
For our fallen
I will always remember

The Great Man
I.D.S
Has passed on
So endeth the link,
of battles fought and won
To sit down and think
Of times past
Of a generation
Who tried to make it last

Every November
I think of dark days past
Comradeship
Duty
Of men
It is these things..
That will always last

Did I ever tell you ?

Did I ever tell you?
Of a time
Of a land
Where we fought
Where we lived
For ideals
When a cause was right
How we never lost
Yet, we faded in to the night

Did I ever tell you?
Of African stars
So bright
As we camped in the bush
Waiting for first light

Did I ever tell you?
Your first contact
The one you remember so vividly
When Mike died
The casevac...
How they tried
They couldn't keep him
The tears
How we all cried...

Did I ever tell you?
Of the bond of men
Sharing our last water
Waiting for resupply
Remember when.......

Did I ever tell you?
That Rhodesians
Are scattered to the four winds
Yet,
Themselves
They remember
The Mikes
The contacts
Of African stars
Of African sky
Of dense bush
The 11th of November
U.D.I

Did I ever tell you?
You cannot destroy
What lies in the heart
Many have tried
Rhodesians survive
Everywhere
We can look back
At a time
Of a land
Where we fought and lived
With pride

That familiar quickening (Part I)

Turbine whistling
Wait...
Until all is green
Time to go

That familiar quickening
Of a heart
Trained in the art of war
To do battle
Rotors spinning

Left and right...
The tech calls
Clear!
Progressive collective
Rising high
In to the sunlight

Time to target
Five minutes
That familiar quickerning
Switches, set

Terrs, visual!
Lynxes, marking with frantan
Left hand orbit
Time to go...

Heave of cyclic
Nose up
Shudder
Bleeding off speed
Safeties , off
You hear the snap and click

In a cloud of dust
A fire force deplaned
For needs must...
Terrs, visual

Max power,
collective to full
Building speed
Skimming trees

Tech, observing
They're running!
Brownings chatter
The cordite smell
The enemy scatter

Watching the fuel
Adjusting throat mike
Ten minutes to bingo
Orbitting
Hearing the battle on the ground
Time to go...

In dusty skies
K-cars and G-cars flew
Skimming across the bush
Purposeful dragonflies
Trained in the art of war

To fight anywhere
That familiar quickening
Turbine whistled
Wait...
Until all is green
Time to go...

That familiar quickening (Part II)

A time for dusk

Enough of fighting for today
We finish our time and duty
For the Lion and Tusk

The blood congealed,
caked with dust
Aching legs,swing round
Dropped clear,
to the ground
On another forward airfield

The long walk back,
to the canteen
The stretching of an aching body
You're late!
Where have you been?

That familiar quickening,
now drained
For, as the sun began to set,
cooling your sweat.
In an African sky,
where battles fought below.
Enough of fighting,
the beer is cold,
the enemy is dead
Let us drink to our lives , instead

The peeling off of stiff camouflage
The days' events,
go through your head
The enemy slain
We lost two men today.......
Tomorrow
We do it all over again.
Let battle commence.....

The Bronze Cross

The siren wailed
The time for killing
Had begun
Let us board our choppers
Go to war
Finish it
Until it is done

I cannot hide
My dread
For, I knew the odds
So many of my friends...
Are dead

Will this be me?
I can, only survive
My training
Carries me through
To manage fear
To stay alive...

I learnt of bravery
Of men
Who were wasted away
Lost for eternity

I learnt of men
Whose actions, I cannot compete
I cocked my FN
The enemy to defeat

I cannot digest
This lust for killing
I have a job to do
Like so many others
They felt this, too

I could not leave
Bob, in all his pain
I carried him
So far
I would do it
In a heartbeat
Again

I would never leave
Any of our men
So, under heavy fire
I carried Bob
I released my fear
I carried him clear

It is all won or lost
On the toss
My circumstances
My training
My comradeship
Carried me
As I carried Bob
For this...
They gave me...
The Bronze Cross

(The men of the R.L.I)

Casevac

You fought to save him
Sosegon, injected in
Drip ,prepared
Pumping for a vein

Pounding his chest
Watching blood droplets spray,
in to the wind
You did your best

Some people die
You cannot save them all
You can but try
Catch them ,before they fall

The Andrew Fleming coming in to view
Attendants ,waiting
Will he survive?
You can only stabilize
Everything you have,
you gave , too

You don't know ,
if the soldier lived or died
You don't have time
You must get busy with the dying
For, the next mission is ready to go
It is the time for flying

The red rust ,
of dried blood and tissue ,
on the chopper floor
A scar for you to see
There is so much more,
with the dying
You must,
put it away
Permanently

To say goodbye...

You died at midday...
As we began the sweep
Down the kopje
Shot three times
The blood
Spilled on to granite
No time to weep

The crackle of gunfire
The deep thump of mortars
We could not help John
There was no time
He was gone

When the contact was over
When we finished our business
Of living for the day
We went back for John
The flies had settled on his drying blood
Upon the granite
Where he lay

There is no dignity
In dying this way
For John...
Upon the granite
Where he lay

We covered his body
With a camouflage jacket
We squatted down
Passed our smokes around

It is not a game
For death will find us
It does not discriminate
We are all the same

We carried John down
Remembering our guilt
Of not dying
Put him on the chopper
Closed our eyes to the dust flying
Soon he was gone

It could have been me
Up there
On the granite
Where John lay
In the suns' glare
Where he lay
Thirty years passed by

I still remember the gunfire
Where he lay
Nothing I could say
Except....
To say goodbye...

The Widow

Rifle fire, echoed
Over your grave
We could not save you
Often ,we prayed
It was never enough
tears, flowed

The love of you
I carry in my heart
The memories too,
always
Who decides who lives?
Who dies?
I cannot understand....
Why they took you.

You promised to be...
so careful
The bitterness inside of me

I see the image of you
In our son
It is a small comfort
That when I needed you the most
You were lost to me
I found it hard to understand
Your sense of duty

Only time
They say
Will heal
Part of me
That they cannot save it.
For, it lies
under echoes
of rifle fire
in your grave

In the loss

In the loss
In the quiet
The Army Chaplain at the door
The, not quite believing
It isn't him
It isn't him

In the loss
The soft words of murmured sympathy
The rituals of tea
In the daze of it all
What it meant to me

Where will I be?
What will I wear
It isn't him
It isn't him
The not quite believing
In the loss

It isn't him
It isn't him
The not quite believing
The Army Chaplain at the door
In the quiet
In the loss

In the dying moments

I held his hand,
in the dying moments
The hardest thing,
to let him go
Yet, I shared the dying moment
His last gift to me
In that closeness
Of a bond
In the dying moment
One day,it will be me

I was with you

I was with you
In that dying moment
I could not bring you back
Nor was I meant to
All I can be
Is with you
You are never alone
In this way
Utterly powerless
I was with you
Yet,that living force is with me
We shared it
The living
The dying
Together
In an intimate moment
I was with you

Deaths' bitter blow

I felt deaths' bitter blow
So little time
So much more to know

If I could just once...
Tell, too...
How much I loved
All of you

I felt deaths' bitter blow
Before I had the chance
To spend more time
With you

I carry a heart
Filled with regret
I had the chance too
To spend more time
With you

I felt deaths' bitter blow
Many wasted times
To tell...
How much I loved
All of you
What I came to know

If I could, just once
For now it is dark
To tell...
So little time now
No time to express
For I feel deaths' bitter blow

If I could, just once
Tell
Of a heart
Filled with regret
So much more to know
It is too late
For I no longer feel
Only deaths' bitter blow

The souvenirs of war

The Government issue brown envelope
Held in my mothers' hands
I knew it was coming ,you see
Nineteen Seventy Eight
I was eighteen
The government , wanted me

The older boys had gone
How they changed in a short six months
That disturbed me
I have dread
Excitement too

I still have that brown envelope,
one of my souvenirs
The other....
A plastic leg
Courtesy of a landmine in a far off T.T.L

Tribal Trust Lands....
Tribal , yes!
Trust, no!
Lands?
That is open to dispute.
Conscription or constriction?
I am not sure which
It is nineteen seventy nine
My national service, given
Not just an arm and a leg
Just a leg....
I feel fortunate it is below the knee.....

The Conscripted Son

The conscripted son
in his hand.......
The unwanted gun

Some were willing.......
Some didn't want the killing
Wasted years
So many tears
They answered the call
So many to fall............

The means to an end
More boys to send......
They cannot see why
They are sent to die

The conscripted son,
in his hand,
the unwanted gun
Blood spilling on the sand

So many came.......
So many died.........
They knew the country's name.......
Rhodesia's fame
Spread far and wide

But now all is lost.......
Was it worth the final cost?
So many to die......
They never found out why

Wounded inside
Scarred outside
Battles won
Wars lost
Lost son
The final cost

The sense of duty
Misused
Abused
No one, won
Everyone lost a son

The Flight of the Lynx

At first light
A Lynx climbed in to the clear sky
In to the sun
So bright

Dawn patrol
Nothing has changed
In over sixty years
The airborne eye

The same T.T.Ls again
Checking kraals and streams
Crap patterns
Spoor from the night rain

Hung beneath camouflaged wings
Sneb rockets
Frantan
Above...
A pair of brownings

Reconnaissance
Everyday
In a blue sky
Standing by...

In the dusty haze
White phosphorous smoke can be seen
Bush fires, everywhere
Burning the green
and open fields of maize

A Lynx..
Behind the suns' glare
Dropped down
Through the air
In its ' hawk like way

Wings flexed,
with the weapons released
Up she rose
Like an Eagle
To the sun
Mission , done

Hard left
Climbing turn
Leaving the target
To burn...

The Alouettes move in for the fight
Dropping off sticks
Time to go
Back to base
Fuel up
Rearm
All in a day
All in a Lynx flight

I was a Selous Scout

Let me tell you....
Of a time
In Rhodesian history
Of a regiment
Bushmen too.....
For, I was a scout
In the tradition of Frederick Courtney Selous
Let me tell you of deeds
What this regiment was about too

In the beginning.....
Men of great heart and commitment
With the love of the bush
By necessity
Formed a regiment
For, an enemy
Will stop at nothing
To destroy all
That belonged to you
To me
We cannot fail

I was a Selous Scout
That lived in twilight
In the bush
Deep in to the enemy stronghold
To search and destroy
Make him lose his will
To give up the fight
In a never never land
When you cannot tell
Who is friend ,who is foe?

You must pit your wits and skill
Become the enemy
Break his will
Set up the kill
In a regiment
Committed to win
Men of black and white
Lived in the twilight world
Of sleight of hand and feint
Such close bonds , you see
Such close ties
Together
To a Regiment
Pamwe Chete

The stories are true
Of a Regiment
Of men
That won medals
For the honour
Pride too
The Grand Cross of Valour
Silver cross
Bronze ones too
For a Regiment
Whose bravery
Of men
Of commitment

Of a Lieutenant Colonels' pride
His vision
The quality of men
To take the fight
To the other side
A Beret of brown
A Silver Osprey
Striking down
Belt of green
The bush man's way

The beginning of the end
When politics lost
Abandoned a regiment
That became a legend
Let me tell you.....
Of a time....
In a Regiment
Of the greatest of men
Who struck deep
In to the hearts of the enemy too
The fading from view
Of a regiment
Who will never forget
The bonds of men
That fought
To the bitter end
Died too.......

I was a Selous Scout
That wore a Beret of Brown
A Silver Osprey
Striking down
Together only
The bonds of men
That fought
Be it, as it may
They will never take the memory
Of a Regiment
A bushman's way

A Hunter was lost

In a Rhodesian sky
Hunters flew
High above
In the blue

With speed and courage
Down, they streaked
Unleashing
All of its' fury
On the enemy

A masterpiece of design
Flown by the chosen few
A Hunter was lost....
In seventy nine

We could not effect..
A recovery...
All that did belong
To a family
To a squadron

So many years
Have passed
Since that terrible day
So many tears

Never again will we hear
That special Hunter sound
Flown by Brian
It does not matter
For now...
He is found

(In memory of Air Lt Brian Gordon 3rd Oct 1979 ,
crash site discovered decades later)

African Moon

In that stillness
Of twilight found
Of dust
Still falling
The fading sounds

In that stillness
Above ghostly Baobabs
In the translucent beauty
The kopjes' granite tops glistened
in the light
of an African Moon

The birds ,fell silent too
In the bright starlit sky
The Milky Way meandered through
Deepest intense blue
The African Moon climbed high

Such beautiful light
Thrown across the sands,
the bush
An African Moon climbed above,
in that night
The rivers' reflected silver light

I dreamed
of that African Moon
In those far off days
In that stillness
Of dust ,falling
and birdsong calling

The Zambesi Valley

30,000 insect species per mile,
half of them in my space
Whirr of wings,
none of which make me smile

Hot foetid air
Decay of leaves
Humidity overwhelms me
I cannot breathe

Dense impenetrable green
Rank pools of water
Holds things, I have never seen

The twitter and call of things unseen
leaves much to the imagination
My wild thrashings,
my curses and condemnation

Leafy clutter abounds every where
Yet nothing is wasted
Nature's powerhouse recycled
Every thing eaten,everything tasted

Dark gloom of triple canopy
Day like night
Night, utter darkness
Terrifies me
For, the Valley, man has no place, no nothing
for the Valley,the insects are king

Frogs croak,hidden things chatter
flash of colour,nothing seen
Stench of decayed matter,
everything green

This moving green mass holds me in its' web
The 30,000 insects,
I dread

Leave,
for the 30,000 insects have evicted me
Don't worry, I will go, you'll see
Whirr of wing
Croak of frog
Escapes me

The faded camouflage

The faded camouflage
So carefully folded away
It was all so sudden
At the end

No troopship to take us back.
No offload of oneself in a six week passage
It was the handing in of rifles
Signing chits for equipment
Never to be used again
There is no glory
Not defeated
Just beaten
Just PTSD

The stink of political defeat
Lay heavy
The unwanted
It would take some years hence
Before reflection
In the glory of living
and the dead

You could always spot the ex-troopie
The short hair
The wasted aggression in the bars
Like the faded camouflage
They too, faded

There is no room in the ZNA
The reminders are too painful to bear
Let it go
Let it go
There is no other way
For, it is lost
Forever

The faded camouflage
Carefully mended
They could not hide all the tears and rips,
of their souls
Those memories, like the faded camouflage
Carefully put away
Hidden
Just like the feelings....

30 Years later.....

I have softened
I remember Kabrit Barracks with fondness
I feel proud of my service
Something to cling on to
The shared bond
We had been through it all
Some lived
Some died
The living, felt like they had died.
I suspect the dead were cheated of the living years

All for a Beige Beret
Who dares ,Wins hey?
I think of selection
I could never do it now
Not the courage , the pain, the fitness

It is easy to be eighteen
You have no fear
No fear at all
I am hitting fifty
Now, I understand fear
Overt and unseen

All of you

So hard you fell
I could never pick up
All the pieces
To make you whole

I gathered all that was left
Blew softly and kissed
Each piece
As though it were your soul

I cannot put it all back
I can, but try
I could never stop your fall
All the pieces too,that I found
What I gathered
Kissed
To make whole
All of you

(A poem to reflect on the mental issues, war can bring)

I am wounded and in the chair

I looked out the window
The light, streaming down
Amongst the trees
Reflecting on me

To walk amongst the trees,
A simple pleasure
Fresh scent of pine
Mind, at ease

I heard birds,
shadows flying from tree to tree
My hand to touch
This roughness of bark
Such thoughts , absurd

How the deepening light,
changes the colour of the trees
I have seen this view
Three thousand and six hundred and fifty times
Memorised it too
Always a delight

The physical bonds that hold me are permanent...
Ten years ago,
the bullets shattered my spine in a contact
The broken back,
shackled me so

I am amongst the trees
I never went away
For, the mind is always free
Living another forest day

I cannot move,
The way I used to
The mind is never chained,
yet in this chair,
my body remained

To walk amongst the trees,
a simple pleasure
Thoughts to treasure
One day....
Please....

I feel,
Yet I cannot touch
The trees
I feel the wind
Blowing through
I wish I could too

Slow silent tears fall,
The light streaming down
Amongst the trees
I never went away
I visited you
every day...

Aftermath

I am still fighting the war
All those years later
Hard roads
Hard times
Only the drink can quench the bitterness that I feel
Was it worth it?
Those men, just wasted
The cause was just
Was it worth it?

I am still fighting the war
All those years later
The glory days
Or were they?
Hard roads
Two divorces later
Those wasted years
Some things cannot be undone
Some things cannot be unseen

The mutilated bodies in kraals
Lips and fingers , chopped off
I am still fighting the war
Only drink can quench the bitterness that I feel
Was it worth it?
I don't know any more.............

I remember the stillness

I remember the stillness
The discipline of quiet
I hold true to that today
Your training never goes away
It is locked in
Available for immediate use

If I could pick up a service rifle
I would know it blindfolded
The satisfying snap of the magazine
Your thumb knows the safety
Automatic memory

Maybe once again
Perhaps down to the range
Playing at contacts
There is still exhilaration
In the discharging of rounds
7.62mm is king
None of that Armalite shit
One bullet ...one death
Economies of scale

I use my government issue green towel
for washing the car
It is still useful

I remember the stillness
When all you could hear was African bush
In the foetid heat of the Zambesi Valley
The discipline of quiet
I hold true to that today
Your training never goes away

Where have they all gone?

The wounded
Without a trace
The many thousands
Who used Tsanga Lodge
Where have they gone?

You cannot erase history
I am truly shocked
At the missing
They should be visible
The reminder of political failure
Where have they gone?

Post script

Did I ever tell you?
You cannot destroy
What lies in the heart
Many have tried
Rhodesians survive
Everywhere
We can look back
At a time
Of a land
Where we fought and lived
With pride

Website

http://aquilamoondust.wix.com/red-sky

Other titles by Author

Poems from the heart
Poems from the heart book 2
A beautiful sky,so red
A beautiful sky,so red A4 size
Beneath a Western sky
Beneath a Western sky A4 size
My colour cosmic sea
My colour cosmic sea A4 size
Beautiful blue world
Beautiful blue world A4 size
The wings of the heart
The wings of the heart A4 size
The Sea and the Sky
The Sea and the Sky A4 size
A river of stars
A river of stars A4 size
The narrow squeak show!
In War and in Battle
The poetry of flowers
Faerie Magick Midnight!
Heart of a storm

In the Moons' reflection
In the Moons' reflection A4 size
Castle Heartstone book 1
Castle Heartstone book 2
Castle Heartstone book 3
Aquila and Moondust
Yellow Moon Sea
A Heartstone Sky
A Heartstone Sky A4 size
Poems for children
Poems for children A4 size
Strange fish and other stories
The Forest Queen
In the Minds' Eye
The Star Tree
The Book of Stars
The Gift Wish
The Star Gift A4 size
The Love of all Things
The Magic of the Trees
The Magic of the Trees A4 size
Golden Heart
Golden Heart A4 size

The Queens of Heartstone
The Queens of Heartstone A4 size
Songs of Water
Songs of Water A4 size
The Place of the Rising Moon
In the light,beautiful things
The Turrets of Sky
Dragonflies and Hearts
Dragonflies and Hearts A4 size
Sails at sunset
Sails at sunset A4 size
In this garden of flowers
In this garden of flowers A4 size
I dreamt of birds
I dreamt of birdsA4 size
The Heartstone Gems
Poetry,that makes men strong
Beautiful,Mystical you
The Autumn King
The Autumn King A4 size
Beacon
Beacon Light A4 size
A Pool of Liquid Night

Night Streams
The Star Catcher
The Star Catcher A4 size
The Tale of a Forest Leaf
The Tale of a Forest Leaf A4 size
The Dreamstone
Cloud light
The Crossing of the Ravens
My Spirit Keeper
Shadowfire
The Sound of Creak
Moon Sky
Aquila Moonfeather
The Golden Light
The Golden Light A4 size
Dragonspark
Amongst the Jewels of her day
Creaks, Trees and Dragonsparks
Remember me
A Cloak of Stars
When one one world slipped away